46

BRITAIN IN PICTURES
THE BRITISH PEOPLE IN PICTURES

BRITISH DRAWINGS

GENERAL EDITOR
W. J. TURNER

The Editor is most grateful to all those who have
so kindly helped in the selection of illustrations
especially to officials of the various public
Museums Libraries and Galleries and
to all others who have generously
allowed pictures and MSS
to be reproduced

BRITISH
DRAWINGS

MICHAEL AYRTON

WITH
8 PLATES IN COLOUR
AND
25 ILLUSTRATIONS IN
BLACK & WHITE

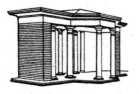

COLLINS · 14 ST. JAMES'S PLACE · LONDON

MCMXLVI

PRODUCED BY
ADPRINT LIMITED LONDON

PRINTED IN GREAT BRITAIN BY
CLARKE & SHERWELL LTD NORTHAMPTON
ON MELLOTEX BOOK PAPER MADE BY
TULLIS RUSSELL & CO LTD MARKINCH SCOTLAND

LIST OF ILLUSTRATIONS

PLATES IN COLOUR

NIMROD SENDING OUT HIS PRINCES FROM BABYLON
&
NIMROD AS A MIGHTY HUNTER
Drawing in three inks on vellum, c. 1000 A.D.
From the Paraphrase of Genesis in MS. Junius 11 in the Bodleian Library

"THE INDUSTRIOUS APPRENTICE PERFORMING THE DUTIES OF A
CHRISTIAN"
Pen and wash sketch by William Hogarth for the engraved series *Industry and Idleness*
published 1747

LANDSCAPE WITH CASTLE
Chalk drawing heightened with white on blue paper by Thomas Gainsborough, 1727-1788

SELF-PORTRAIT, 1776
Red chalk drawing by Allan Ramsay, 1713-1784

THE CHIMNEY PIECE
Wash drawing by Henry Fuseli, 1741-1825

SNOWDON UNDER CLOUD, 1853
Pen and wash drawing by James Ward, 1769-1859

JOACHIM AMONG THE SHEPHERDS, 1912
Pen and wash drawing by Stanley Spencer, b. 1892

TWO SISTERS, 1945
Drawing in coloured chalks by Robert Colquhoun, b. 1914

BLACK AND WHITE ILLUSTRATIONS

PAGE

DR. MISAUBIN AND DR. WARD 5
Pen, pencil and wash drawing by William
Hogarth, 1697-1764
By gracious permission of H.M. The King

LANDSCAPE WITH A DARK HILL 7
Aquatint worked over in pencil and wash
by Alexander Cozens, d. 1786
By courtesy of Sir Edward Marsh

THREE LADIES 9
Brush point sketch from a notebook of
Thomas Gainsborough, 1727-1788
By courtesy of Sir Robert Witt

GUTHLAC AT THE MOUTH OF HELL 11
Line drawing from the *Life of St. Guthlac
of Croyland*. Late twelfth century (Harley
Roll, Y.6)
By courtesy of the Trustees of the British Museum

THREE APOSTLES SEATED: PAGE FROM A
SKETCHBOOK IN THE PEPYSIAN LIBRARY 13
Metal point and brush drawing of the late
fourteenth century
*By courtesy of the Librarian of Magdalene College,
Cambridge*

COURT LADY 15
Pen drawing by Nicholas Hillyarde,
c. 1547-1619
*By courtesy of the Director of the Victoria & Albert
Museum*

CARICATURE 18
Pen drawing by Isaac Oliver, 1556-1617
By courtesy of Thomas Lowinsky, Esq.

HEAD OF A BOY 19
Pen drawing by Inigo Jones, 1573-1652
By courtesy of Thomas Lowinsky, Esq.

MAN WITH A DOG 21
Pen drawing by Francis Barlow, c. 1626-
1704
By courtesy of Thomas Lowinsky, Esq.

DESIGN FOR A CEILING 23
Pen and wash drawing by Sir James
Thornhill, 1675-1734
By courtesy of Sir Robert Witt

THE SPIRIT OF GOD 26
Wash drawing by George Romney, 1734-
1802
*By courtesy of the Trustees of the Fitzwilliam
Museum, Cambridge*

ENRAGED MAN 28
Pen drawing by Thomas Rowlandson,
1756-1827
By courtesy of Thomas Lowinsky, Esq.

THE ANCIENT OF DAYS 29
Drawing by William Blake, 1757-1827
By courtesy of Thomas Lowinsky, Esq.

PAGE

RUTH RETURNED FROM GLEANING 31
Chalk and wash drawing by Samuel
Palmer, exhibited 1829
*By courtesy of the Director of the Victoria & Albert
Museum*

VIEW ON THE STOUR 33
Wash drawing by John Constable, c. 1820
*By courtesy of the Director of the Victoria & Albert
Museum*

ROCKY COAST WITH PORT 35
Pen and water colour drawing by Richard
Dadd, 1861
By courtesy of the Trustees of the British Museum

WOMAN ON A SOFA 36
Pen drawing by Sir David Wilkie, 1805
By courtesy of Thomas Lowinsky, Esq.

SPANISH MODEL 37
Pen drawing by Charles Keene, 1823-1891
By courtesy of Thomas Lowinsky, Esq.

MISS FANNY CORNFORTH 38
Pen and wash drawing by Dante Gabriel
Rossetti, 1828-1882
By courtesy of the Leicester Galleries, London

NIGHT PIECE 39
Pen and brush drawing by Aubrey
Beardsley, 1872-1898
By courtesy of Louis C. G. Clarke, Esq.

SEATED WOMAN 43
Pen and wash drawing by Wyndham
Lewis
By courtesy of the Artist and the Leicester Galleries

THE LONDON, SHOREDITCH 44
Pencil drawing by Walter Richard Sickert,
1860-1942
By courtesy of the Leicester Galleries

STUDY OF A FISHERGIRL OF EQUIHEN 45
Pencil drawing by Augustus John
By courtesy of the Artist and the Hon. John Freman

ORCHARD 47
Pen and wash drawing by John Minton,
1945
By courtesy of the Artist and Dr. H. Roland

THORNTREE 48
Pen and wash drawing by Graham
Sutherland, 1945
By courtesy of the Artist

COVER DESIGN

BATTLEPIECE: A CAVALRY ENGAGEMENT
Line drawing by Mathew Paris, d. 1259,
illustrating his *Romance of the Two Offas*
(Cotton MS. Nero D.1)
By courtesy of the Trustees of the British Museum

LANDSCAPE WITH A DARK HILL
Aquatint worked over in pencil and wash by Alexander Cozens, d. 1786

ARGUMENT

THE vexed question of the merits and demerits of nationalism in art is forced upon anyone who writes specifically, as this book requires, on the product of a single nation. There is a case to be made against conscious nationalism, on the grounds that it leads to parochialism and that such a conception is in any case spurious, art being on a plane above the politics which the word "nationalism" seems to imply. My own view is that the value of nationalism stands in direct ratio to the strength of a culture at a given time. The power to benefit from outside influence is in fact commensurate with the ability to refrain from being totally dominated by it. When the creative state of a nation is low but gradually improving, consciousness of, and pride in, a native tradition is valuable. Equally when a culture is in the ascendant, the participants therein can afford to welcome foreign influence and gain from it. The fact that a national tradition has existed and been of great importance during certain of the periods covered by this book, is obvious ; that there is a continuity

7

in the progression of British art, and in particular drawing, I hope to show. Its value is a matter of opinion.

This continuity is perhaps not easy to follow, nor is it uninterrupted ; during one long period badly so: but unlike that of nations whose flame has been far brighter, this island's flickering torch has continued to burn spasmodically for a thousand years. Italy produced a gigantic succession of masters between Giotto and the death of Titian and then surrendered to a subsequent, almost unrelieved, triviality ; the great Gothic art of Flanders died out ; Holland, during the century of her maritime power, produced a school, of which Rembrandt is the culmination, which exercised an enormous influence long after the source had dried up ; and so on. Great Britain has produced no Michelangelo, no Van Eyck and no Rembrandt ; but neither have we ceased to be creative nor do we show any signs of ceasing to be. Perhaps this is because the culmination has not yet been reached. At certain times, circumstances and the domination of particular foreign influences have come so near to smothering native talent as to create every appearance of a desert left barren by mighty conquerors, but the essential qualities have somehow survived, more often in drawing than in other forms of expression. The native qualities themselves, the varying influences brought to bear upon them over a period of one thousand years and the value of British drawing in relation to the European tradition —the value in short of a national culture—form the argument of this essay. The exchange value of a culture is the true coin of "internationalism" in art, for it is by the exchange of cultures between nations that art becomes international. I have therefore included among the reproductions practically no "foreigners working in England" as the British Museum Catalogue defines them, for they usually appeared in their might at times when we were least calculated to benefit from them. Fuseli is an exception because, in my view, Fuseli was *plus royaliste que le roi*, an English artist. He was an interesting if minor practitioner, and he very fully assimilated the British idiom of his time, which could not have been said, for instance, of Holbein or Kneller. The choice of reproductions is inevitably a personal one, sadly limited by the size of the volume, and will probably be unpopular. I have endeavoured to include a reasonable number of drawings by the greatest of our painters and a certain number by artists whose drawings I feel have been unjustly neglected. I have also given considerable space to illustrations from pre-sixteenth century manuscripts on the grounds that one of our greatest contributions to European art was made in this form of drawing and in that age. I have tried to reproduce examples of as many as possible of the various media—chalk, pencil, pen, wash, etc.—which come within the scope of drawing *per se* as opposed to the other vehicles of visual expression. Those artists whose drawing is only relevant to their work in oil or watercolour *painting* (as opposed to the tinted drawing) such as Turner and the Norwich school of landscape painters, I have sacrificed, admirable

8

NIMROD SENDING OUT HIS PRINCES FROM BABYLON
&
NIMROD AS A MIGHTY HUNTER

Drawing in three inks on vellum, c.1000 A.D.

From the Paraphrase of Genesis in MS. Junius 11 in the Bodleian Library

"THE INDUSTRIOUS APPRENTICE PERFORMING THE DUTIES OF A CHRISTIAN"
Pen and wash sketch by William Hogarth for the engraved series *Industry and Idleness* published 1747

though their topographical drawings are, to others such as Francis Barlow, Alexander Cozens and Charles Keene whose drawings are their finest work, since this book is primarily concerned with draughtsmen rather than with painters. At the same time I have, I hope, reproduced a sufficient number of "painters' drawings" to give an indication of this essential aspect of the practice of drawing. Topographical drawings deserve a volume to themselves and I can only plead lack of space if they are ill represented in this one. Apart from drawings made for purposes of study and in preparation for work in other media, there have been a large number of drawings made for the sake of drawing, as being the form of expression most suited to the particular conception. In my opinion the continuity to which I have referred is more easily traceable in the use of the intimate medium of drawing than in painting or any other means of pictorial expression. Furthermore this country's pictorial genius has always been primarily a genius for drawing.

THREE LADIES
Brush point sketch by Thomas Gainsborough, 1727-1788

ASCENDANCY

BRITISH drawing as such may be said to start in the tenth century, following the decay of the Carlovingian Empire, and the chaos resulting from its collapse. Prior to this, and indeed prior to the empire of Charlemagne itself, masterpieces of illumination had been created in Ireland and Northumbria of which the Book of Kells and the Lindisfarne Gospels are probably the most famous extant examples. In these books the Celtic gift for abstract designs and ornament is seen in its most highly developed form, but this aspect of art does not come within the immediate scope of this book, though the enduring influence of Celtic pattern-making runs through the succeeding centuries. Towards the end of the Carlovingian epoch the Danish invaders of England demolished a large proportion of pre-ninth century manuscripts and contemporary work ceased. That much was destroyed, is recorded by King Alfred who "saw, before it was ravaged and burnt, how the churches throughout the whole of England stood filled with treasures and books." To all intents and purposes, this essay in history begins with our recovery from this period of devastation.

Charlemagne was dead and his empire speedily disintegrated. In the general shake-up naturally following upon the collapse of the centralised government, separate imperialist states were established throughout Europe which eventually gave birth to distinct and independent cultures, but it was an energetic and international programme of monastic reform, as part of a period of reorganisation and reconstruction not entirely dissimilar to the present one, which was directly responsible for the maintenance of a European tradition, and incidentally led to the rebirth of British art. Why the splendid phenomenon of the "Winchester School" sprang into existence so suddenly and in such a degree of apparent maturity is not known, nor indeed is it quite certain in what parts of England the Winchester School originated, but within a few years of St. Dunstan being made Archbishop of Canterbury and St. Æthelwold Bishop of Winchester, there existed at Winchester a style of drawing which was both original and highly evolved. The basis of this style is traceable to Carlovingian models and also owed a good deal to the insular tradition of Northumbrian ornament, which had been continued and indeed closely followed by the Franco-Saxon school throughout the Carlovingian era, but the detail, the extraordinary nervous vitality and linear freedom of the Winchester drawings was something entirely new. By the eleventh century this renaissance had spread to include Canterbury and Bury St. Edmunds as centres of production, and it is from a manuscript, probably of Canterbury, that the first colour plate of the present volume is taken. This manuscript, called the Cædmon, and written in Anglo-Saxon, contains illustrated poems on biblical themes. The present illustration is thought by one authority to represent "Nimrod sending out his princes to enlarge his boundaries" and "Nimrod as a mighty hunter before the Lord." Another equally learned scholar considers it to be "Cush or his son ruling his tribe" and "The Hebrews departing with their cattle." The reader may take his choice but for my part, I favour Nimrod. What is of greater interest is the vigorous lyricism of the drawings themselves which could hardly be more remote from the monumental rigidity of the Byzantine mode current in Southern Europe, nor from the grandiose stolidity of Ottonian art, then at its height in Germany. The drawings of this and the succeeding two centuries, with their precise, rhythmic use of line, line that spurts and darts like a bird, are the touchstone of British drawing. The same lyrical qualities, the same rhythmic preoccupations, appear over and over again in our subsequent history

GUTHLAC AT THE MOUTH OF HELL
Line drawing from the *Life of St. Guthlac of Croyland*. Late twelfth century

The lively condition of British art in the eleventh century was such that the arrival, following "the Conquest," of Norman scribes and monks, bringing with them their sumptuous French manner of illumination, merely added weight and strength to the existing convention without materially altering the original linear manner already being employed. The famous masterpiece of the period, the "Winchester Bible," contains superb examples of the marriage of the two schools and also is an instance of the astonishing ability with which several artists of unified purpose could, over a considerable number of years, combine their individual styles to produce a single great work of art. The major continental innovation of the twelfth century, the "Albani Psalter" style, produced a strong Anglo-Romanesque synthesis which checked the affectation towards which the Anglo-Saxon manner had been tending, without substantially changing the method of outline drawing employed. Towards the end of the twelfth century, a new form of illustrated book came into vogue, derived mainly from the *"Etymologiae" of Isidore of Seville*. This was the Bestiary, virtually an English invention, in which fabulous creatures and familiar animals were portrayed indulging in various probable and improbable activities. This form of popular illustration presaged a long tradition of artists specialising in drawings of animals and birds, which has continued in its course to the present day. At much the same time, the easily portable illustrated Psalter became popular, a fashion which was to last until the end of the fourteenth century, and such Psalters were exported in sufficient numbers to spread the influence of the British school throughout France and much of Europe. By the thirteenth century, the rich but heavy Anglo-Norman manner had gradually given way to a revival of the linear delicacy found in Anglo-Saxon drawings, the earliest separate "Books of Hours" were produced, and these were followed by a long series of illustrated Apocalypses and histories. It is in this period that individual artists begin to be known by name ; William de Brailes contrived to sign a Psalter, and the celebrated Mathew Paris, historiographer to the Abbey of St. Albans, friend of Henry III, diplomat, gold engraver, author, cartographer and draughtsman, achieved personal fame. A fair number of Mathew Paris's drawings has survived, though no signed ones, and even a certain amount of his personal history is known to us. It is recorded that he was "a religious monk," very highly esteemed at St. Albans, and that he undertook an unusual mission to Norway for the King and left his influence as an artist behind him there. His principal surviving drawings are in his *Historia Maior* now at Cambridge, in another history now in the British Museum and in his *Romance of the Two Offas*. He left a considerable school behind him when he died in 1259, whose work is not easy to distinguish from his own.

The reputation of British drawing and illumination was now of European stature, British illustrated books were in the hands of the courts of most of Europe and Englishmen were working in Paris, creating the Anglo-French school of painting which was eventually to dominate Northern Europe. Near the end of the thirteenth century the centre of productivity had moved to Peterborough, where the artists themselves had ceased to be monastic and were chiefly professional laymen. Humorous decoration is a feature of the East Anglian School ; on the borders of sacred pages, fabulous beasts in combat with zoomorphs, which foreshadow the demonologies of Jerome Bosch, are gaily combined with pastoral scenes from everyday life; familiar domestic animals in the tradition of the earlier Bestiaries.

In 1348 production seems to have ceased abruptly for twenty years. The reasons for this are unknown, though possibly the Black Death

THREE APOSTLES SEATED: PAGE FROM A SKETCHBOOK IN THE PEPYSIAN LIBRARY
Metal point and brush drawing of the late fourteenth century

was responsible, but from henceforward there is a general decline in the excellence of British work which corresponds with the rise of France to supremacy in the field of illumination. A revival took place during the second part of the fourteenth century chiefly as a result of the patronage of the Bohun family, five of whose commissioned books have come down to us, and there are a few missals and lectionaries of the period, which are of more than historical interest. One of these latter (Harley MS. 7026), illustrated under the direction of one John Syfrewas, contains one of the earliest known examples of genuine portraiture in this country ; a deliberate attempt at the likeness of John, 5th Lord Loval. Earlier drawings are concerned with idealised generalisations, rather than with individual portraits, since the status of a rank in medieval times was considered more important artistically than the holder of it. The supposed self-portrait of de Brailes in the Last Judgement leaf of a Psalter (Fitzwilliam Museum, Cambridge) is an idealised figure who is being rescued from damnation by St. Michael. The figure holds a scroll inscribed "W. de Brail me f(e)cit."

One of the most interesting survivals of late fourteenth century drawing is the volume, now in the Pepysian Library at Cambridge, called "The

Monk's Draw : Book." This medieval sketch book contains, as the work of several, probably secular, hands, a variety of figure and animal drawings, some of which are charming, some extremely clumsy. These were possibly prepared as studies for manuscript illustration, sculpture, or the form of embroidery known as "Opus Anglicanum" which was justly famed throughout Europe. But the rot had set in. During the fifteenth century France was producing such masterpieces as *Les Très Riches Heures du Duc de Berry*; the *Hours of Elizabeth the Quene*, England's finest fifteenth century achievement, cannot be said to rival it. British art was in decline and though a few charming drawings were made by Englishmen at the time, notably by John Rows in his history of the Earls of Warwick called the "Warwick Roll," French and Flemish artists were being imported into England in large numbers and were doing better work than our own. Unlike the period following the Norman Conquest, there was no strength left in British art to assimilate and transpose the powerful influence. For reasons never satisfactorily established, perhaps the anarchy of the Wars of the Roses, perhaps the renewed Black Death, or possibly the inevitable cyclical decline of national artistic virility, the fifteenth century saw the end of this great phase of British drawing. We were not to rise again to a position of international repute for three hundred years.

I would like to digress here to comment upon the actual media in which the drawings, so far discussed, were executed. Fine vellum was the usual surface, for though paper had been made in Spain since the eleventh century and was in use in several parts of Europe from then on, there is no record of its manufacture in England before the fifteenth century. Wynkyn de Worde was the first to mention an English paper mill in his edition of *De Proprietatibus Rerum* printed *c.* 1495. Vellum was in any case a finer surface for delicate drawing. The methods employed in working on vellum allowed some variation. The Norman scribes had imported the heavy body colour in which the subsequent illuminations were frequently worked, but before this, pure line drawings in several colours, made with reed or quill pens and sometimes shaded with the point of a brush, had been deemed complete illustrations in themselves, as in the Cædmon MS. The twelfth century Winchester Bible contains examples of several different techniques. Those which concern us in this book, the line drawings, were usually made in chalk or in lead point, an earlier and more difficult tool than its later development, the pencil. The variation in the method employed depended on whether the design was intended to be heavily overpainted, in which case it was left as an exceedingly delicate indication. Alternatively, if the intention was merely to wash transparent colour over drawn line, as in those by the "Master of the Apocrypha Drawings," the point was used precisely and pressed heavily. A quite remarkable number of drawings in medieval manuscripts were left uncoloured, in their original state as line drawings.

COURT LADY
Pen drawing by Nicholas Hillyarde, c. 1547-1619

THE DESERT

IT has never been possible to establish any very definite reason for the
rise and fall of artistic temperatures, but economic and religious circumstances doubtless play their part. The Dissolution of the Monas-
teries, which had for so long been the patron of our arts, and the visual
philistinism of the new king, who systematically destroyed most of the

medieval works of art he laid his hands on, did in effect administer the *coup de grâce* to the already feeble body of British art, but to all intents and purposes the patient was already beyond hope before any of these contingencies arose. The establishment of the Church of England as part of the Reformation, effectively prevented our taking any part in the evolution of the Baroque which was essentially a Catholic phenomenon and part of the Roman reply to the Lutheran heresy, but it will remain an open question whether anything but the most sedulous nursing of the native tradition following the accession of Henry VIII would have kept the thing alive. Needless to say, not only did this fail to occur but the arrival on the English scene of Hans Holbein the younger as court painter was a final blow. Remarkable though Holbein's own drawings were, his followers were few and his influence was negative mainly because his methods were archaic even in his own day. For nearly a century there are no British drawings of the slightest interest by English followers of Holbein. It might reasonably have been suggested at the time that the native tradition was extinct ; as dead in fact as Charlemagne. This gloomy situation continued unrelieved. Flemish portrait painters such as Antonio Moro were well received, but the domestic product was treated with scorn. That no one called Smith, Brown or Bossam had the slightest chance of earning a living is made abundantly clear in the following quotation from *A Treatise concerning the Art of Limning* by the miniaturist, or 'limner,' Nicholas Hillyarde. "The most rare English drawer," says he, "of English story works in black and white, John Bossam for one of his skill worthy to have been Sergant Painter to any King or Emperour, whose work in that kind are comparable with the best whatsoever in cloathe in distemper cullors for white or black ; who being very poore and belyke wanting to by faier cullors, wrought therefore for the most part in white and black and growing yet poorer by charge of children etc., gave painting cleane over." The wretched and talented Bossam, none of whose work survives, became a "reading minister" for his living. "*He was*" Hillyarde continues "*only unfortunate because he was English born, for even the strangers would otherwise have set him upp.*" The italics are mine and are made with considerable bitterness. The Elizabethan dilettantes' belief in the inevitable superiority of continental art bears a striking resemblance to our own day and age. "Our courtiers and great personages," wrote Henry Peacham, (*Graphice* 1606), "must seeke farre and neere for some Dutchman or Italian to draw their pictures and invent their deuices, our Englishmen being held for Vaunients" (good-for-nothings). Peacham probably knew what he was talking about for he was a draughtsman himself in addition to his journalistic activities. Hillyarde was lucky in that he died in only comparative poverty, and lived tolerably well as Limner to Queen Elizabeth, though "brought into great extremes" in 1599. Two drawings by him exist, apart from his exquisite miniatures in opaque water colours. One of these drawings is his design in

LANDSCAPE WITH CASTLE
Chalk drawing heightened with white on blue paper by Thomas Gainsborough, 1727-1788
By courtesy of Messrs. Roland, Browse & Delbanco

SELF-PORTRAIT

Red chalk drawing by Allan Ramsay, 1776

pen over black chalk, for the Queen's Great Seal ; the other, a delicate pen drawing of a court lady, is reproduced here.

There is a much larger body of drawings by Hillyarde's pupil, Isaac Oliver, a fair number of brush drawings in black and white on coloured paper, some elegant portraits and a few lively caricatures. Oliver was French and Huguenot by birth but came to England as a young child, and spent his life here, for which reason he may be considered a British draughtsman, in that he was not simply a visitor, with a made reputation, come for pickings.

Nicholas Hillyarde himself was influenced by Holbein's miniatures and is the solitary important exception to that master's otherwise negative legacy. He was also a passionate admirer of the Italians and of Albert Dürer's drawings, but his quality is essentially native to this island in an age otherwise conspicuously barren as far as the pictorial is concerned. His exquisitely lyrical talent is the only visual equivalent of the poetic gifts of his literary contemporaries, and he is perhaps the only great English artist of Tudor and Stuart times. Whatever others there might have been were probably forced into other walks of life ("unfortunate because English born") before they had the opportunity to prove their worth. Only one other artist of the times, though certainly not a great one, is worthy of mention: John White, who combined the somewhat arduous activity of governing Raleigh's "second colonie" of Virginia, with drawing, and painting in water colours. He is seen at his best in his drawings of reptiles and animals, but his figure drawings are full of vigour if rather unskilful. What work of White's survives, is in the form of an album, recording his sojourn in America, and is now in the British Museum.

The Jacobean period has little to recommend it and in the reign of Charles I, like that of Henry VIII, Great Britain was, artistically, simply an "occupied country," though it must be said that Charles, unlike Henry, was a man of taste. Foreign artists completely dominated portraiture, which continued to be the major pictorial activity. Rubens visited England at the King's invitation and Van Dyck, his pupil, who was a visitor in 1620, returned and settled here as court painter in 1635 to become, not unnaturally, the most admired master draughtsman in the country. What English followers he had were, for the most part, *pasticheurs* of very little merit. Samuel Cooper is of more interest than his contemporaries, for it was Cooper who, allowing for the change of style relevant to his time, carried on the miniaturist tradition of Hillyarde with something like the same excellence. His drawings are very rare.

The English master draughtsman who really dominates the domestic scene after Hillyarde's death is Inigo Jones, the architect and stage designer. Jones studied landscape painting in Italy, turned to architecture and, between 1605 and 1640, produced a stream of designs for costumes, scenery and stage machinery for masques and operas, in addition to his architectural

achievements as "Master of the King's Worke." It cannot be pretended that Jones was an obviously English artist in manner, since the influence of Italy was always foremost in his work, but his drawings have a spontaneity which far removes them from the general run of contemporary British work. His virtue in all his activities lay in his ability to adapt foreign, particularly Palladian, idioms to English usage. His drawings are mostly in pen and wash.

Peter Lely, who had arrived in the year of Van Dyck's death, succeeded his countryman as the fashionable portraitist of the next forty years, produced a monotonous series of third-rate portrait drawings, which became steadily worse, and an equally monotonous set of followers, of whom John Greenhill was the most sensitive and able.

The Commonwealth, as everyone knows, was more concerned with destroying graven images than with encouraging the creation of such baubles as drawings. The Ironsides went into battle with bible and sword and, during interim periods, passed happy hours burning early illustrated editions of the former and slashing the supreme achievement of medieval wall painting with the latter. On the whole I imagine, they completed Henry VIII's task of nation-wide vandalism to their own satisfaction. Iconophobia is a disease to which England has been tragically subject at intervals. During the Commonwealth, however, mediocre portrait drawing continued, there being no grounds for theological dispute over sternly dull portrayals of puritans, and by the Restoration a larger number of British artists appear to have been in practice, among whom John Riley was the most talented painter. Topographical drawing had been introduced by the Bohemian, Wenzel Hollar, and was in some demand. Hollar's friend, Francis Place, the first Englishman to employ mezzotint in engraving, is one of the earliest, and by no means the least, of a long line of English topographical draughtsmen, but it was another friend of Hollar and also of Place whose work is the best indication of the survival of the indigenous tradition at this period. This was Francis Barlow, the bird and animal draughtsman, who followed the special tradition which, originating in "the Bestiary," had managed to survive in the applied arts of embroidery, masonry and ceramic, while the fine arts lay dormant. Barlow's drawings, particularly of birds, bear a striking resemblance to thirteenth century marginalia without being in the least archaic. He drew and engraved most of the rural activities connected with animals and his illustrations for Aesop's *Fables* are justly celebrated. The drawing here reproduced is a good example of his fresh, pastoral style. Meanwhile in portraiture Lely and the unsuccessful but gifted Riley were to some extent overshadowed by the arrival in England of an even more tedious figure, Gottfried Kneller, whose vogue was to last, as a result of his business acumen, until his death in the year of Joshua Reynold's birth.

HEAD OF A BOY
Pen drawing by Inigo Jones, 1573-1652

For all the continued supremacy of the visitors from abroad, an increasing number of British artists are in evidence, most of them either miniaturists or portrait draughtsmen. Greenhill, Loggan, Fairthorne, Thrumton, Forster, Lutterel, Robert White, Mary Beale and her son Charles were all contriving to earn their daily bread. Whilst their individual works are not very impressive, they were all tolerably proficient and may at all events be given the credit for being part of the soil in which the eighteenth century flowers were to take root.

On paper of various colours, the principal media in which these portraitists worked were red and black chalk, and plumbago—a form of graphite pencil very similar to the modern article. Graphite was known as early as the sixteenth century but did not come into very general use, except in this isolated period, until the early nineteenth century when Brockendon's method of compressing powdered black lead produced the pencil as we know it. The principal form these drawings took was studies for painting, and the facsimile engravings which were now finding a fair market. Highly finished chalk and plumbago portraits were sold independently to those who could not afford, or did not want, oil paintings. The drawings of Barlow and those of the early topographers are principally in bistre, a brown ink prepared from beechwood soot, worked in pen and wash. The word "sepia" now generally applied to early drawings of a brownish hue is a misnomer. Sepia, the dye of the cuttlefish, does not seem to have been used before the eighteenth century. The brown colour of many early draw-ings is due either to bistre or to the fading of iron gall ink which would have been black when originally applied. Pastel colours had been introduced from France before the Restoration and were used in Riley's time. Accord-ing to Horace Walpole, one Edmund Ashfield had considerably increased the colour range of the medium during the latter half of the century, and Evelyn the diarist speaks of portraits of his cousin's children "all painted in one piece, very well, by Mr. Luttrel in crayon on copper" (4.8.1694).

RESURRECTION

THE very early years of the eighteenth century were of that darkness popularly supposed to precede the dawn, and a Stygian gloom it was. Jones was dead and Barlow died in 1702. The portraitists are represented by the secondary gifts of the Richardsons, father and son. Jonathan Richardson, the elder, had been a pupil of Riley, and being talented, had succeeded Kneller as the fashionable purveyor of the aristo-cratic visage. A solitary British exponent of the late Baroque, Sir James Thornhill, was much in demand as a decorator, particularly of ceilings in great country houses and public buildings. Thornhill drew in the florid, somewhat grandiose manner of Tiepolo and the late Venetians. Usually a second-rate performer, there is a certain dash and brilliance in the best of his drawings. His work is almost always in direct relation to architecture and is at least exceedingly accomplished. Pen, wash and chalk were not unnaturally the media he employed.

The dawn however was breaking in no uncertain fashion. In 1697, William Hogarth, who is generally supposed to be the father of all British art, but who actually was the symbol of its reawakening rather than its birth, was born in London, and within twenty years Scotland had produced Allan Ramsay, and Wales, Richard Wilson. The century following these events is generally considered the great period of British painting and it is certainly one of the two peaks of our achievement in drawing. The thin trickle of the preceding two hundred years from the magnificent, if cloudy, sources of the Gothic period now widens into a river, comprising three main streams which, though superficially different, in essence show the same virtues as the source. The lyrical vision of the tenth and eleventh centuries is reasserted in the drawings of Gainsborough, Alexander Cozens and Richard Wilson, though the form has become principally landscape immediately subject to Italian, Dutch and French influences. The linear vitality and freedom of the early Winchester school re-emerges in the hands of Hogarth and Rowlandson while the visionary imagination of the Gothic draughtsmen reappears in the work of Blake and his circle. Hogarth's direct

MAN WITH A DOG
Pen drawing by Francis Barlow, c. 1626-1704

derivations as a draughtsman are not easy to place ; his method of using the pen was with a loose, spontaneous and even wavering line; the result being then rapidly washed over with tone in brush. In manner his drawings are rather Italianate, presumably as a result of his training under his future father-in-law, Thornhill, and he must have seen, in the collection of Dr. Richard Mead, the drawings and paintings of Antoine Watteau, the greatest continental visitor since Rubens. There is a direct historical link between Watteau and Hogarth, in the person of a dubious medical practitioner, a Dr. Misaubin, whom Watteau drew when he was in London in 1719 (engraved by Arthur Pond) and whom Hogarth pilloried in "Marriage *à la mode*" and in the small drawing reproduced. But Hogarth's drawings, if they have something in common with Tiepolo's caricatures and occasionally a Watteauesque elegance, have also a burly shrewdness and freedom which are his own. He had no great admiration for the Dutch, and indeed he caricatured what he called the "vulgar" Dutch fashion in "Paul before Felix," an engraving "designed and scratched in the true Dutch taste," a mockery of

Steen, Ostade and Rembrandt but also of his own failure to achieve "the grand manner." Nevertheless if a parallel is to be found for Hogarth as a draughtsman it is in the work of such "vulgar" artists as Pieter Breughel the elder and the Dutch engravers. Most of Hogarth's extant drawings are rapid notes for engravings (like the colour plate) but there are also some portrait drawings such as the famous pencil and wash study of Lord Lovat, before his execution for treason, in the Pierpont Morgan Library. In Hogarth's *Analysis of Beauty*, the textbook he wrote "with a view to fixing the fluctuating ideas of taste," which was so scorned in his own day and is of so much interest in ours, he explains the mysterious winding line drawn on the palette in his famous self-portrait. It is the "line of beauty," the curve which he considered should be present in all good art. Whatever may have been thought by his contemporaries of the line itself, Hogarth, in his preoccupation with it, follows in the long, indigenous tradition. The main stream to which Hogarth belongs as a draughtsman is the popular form of drawing which runs from the humorous and satirical marginalia of the Peterborough manuscripts, and includes Rowlandson, Gilray, Cruikshank, Keene, and a host of lesser figures—by no means the very least of which is our own contemporary, the cartoonist "Giles"—whose mode of existence depends on the cheap engraving and whose concern is the everyday trials of the common man and the bitter comedies of "high life." Every nation and occasion produces this form of social comment in one way or another and it is perhaps the most obviously "national" form of drawing. Hogarth's significance in the history of art is to be found in his attitude to daily life—he was (as R. H. Wilenski says in his *English Painting*) "a man with the social conscience which the English nation was about to develop more and more."

Allan Ramsay is a complete contrast. As a man, he was a gentle, courtly individual, more interested in a pleasant and intellectual life than in his art; as a draughtsman, in his use of chalk, he bears a greater resemblance to Gainsborough than to his own immediate contemporaries. What he had was great delicacy of perception, an unusual attribute among British artists of his day, and a poetic sensitivity which gave his portrait drawings much grace. His drawings, like certain of Gainsborough's, recall Watteau, whose work Ramsay would have seen at Dr. Mead's. There is no doubt that Watteau was the most beneficial foreign influence, as far as figure drawing is concerned, on the British art of this period; that his influence was undoubtedly a good one, was in no small measure due to our rejuvenated ability to accept and benefit from it. A decade earlier, we might well have suffered from it.

As a profession, portraiture remained the staple provider. The British nobleman, as the eighteenth century progressed, gradually took to employing his own countrymen to immortalise his features, but he was more dilatory in encouraging native landscape painting. He preferred, or it was fashionable, to own landscapes in the Roman manner by Claude rather than those

DESIGN FOR A CEILING
Pen and wash drawing by Sir James Thornhill, 1675-1734

of Richard Wilson which were not entirely dissimilar, but Wilson was of a prickly disposition and had undoubted originality which motivated against his success. To quote R. H. Wilenski again, Wilson "was never content to be a *pasticheur* but tended to break the mould of the [Italian] tradition by a more naturalistic and romantic approach." This tendency is remarkable

23

even earlier in his drawings than in his oil paintings. His drawings are principally in black chalk on tinted paper, of a greater freedom and less sharply defined than those of either Claude or Gaspar Poussin. The natural lyricism of his landscape conception was not at home with the rigorous conventions of the classical style and in this he preceded Gainsborough and Constable, the most lyrical of all our landscape painters. Wilson himself studied in Italy and, except in his late work, the Italian influence is usually present in some degree, but he was the first to cast off the complete domination of continental methods of landscape practice.

British landscape drawing absorbed, and turned to its own particular use, a combination of the Flemish topographical tradition, the French or Franco-Italian conception of the classical-sublime landscape and the Dutch conception of the picturesque landscape. This latter was more congenial to those who followed Wilson than the hidebound formulae of the classical and sublime. It was concerned with the particulars of nature rather than the generalities of art. It was romantic, and the romantic is our natural element in landscape. Alexander Cozens was also trained in Italy and also reacted against classicism. Unlike Wilson, far and away the most important of Cozens' works are his drawings, and particularly his wash drawings. He made curiously dry topographical studies of Italian scenes in pen, but he also devised a method of splashing bistre wash on to paper, more or less arbitrarily, and selecting forms and combinations from the blots, which he would then work up with a brush into landscapes of a sombre and powerful kind. Alexander Cozen's influence is present in Turner's water colours, and Turner admits to having used his "blot method." In a sense therefore Cozens is an early forerunner of nineteenth century French Impressionism. The drawing illustrated is worked in pencil and wash over a basis of aquatint, either as the correction of a "state," or because Cozens found the texture an interesting basis for his method. In any case it is a perfect example of the romantic landscape drawing. Alexander's son, John Robert Cozens, is more famous as a watercolourist. He was not, I think, the equal of his father as a draughtsman, but at least, during his short life, he managed to pass on what he had learnt from his father and to produce drawings of considerable charm though lacking the parental imaginative power.

In one aspect of our painting, the "sporting picture," for which all too few studies remain, the maintenance of a level of accuracy in the presentation of the whole subject required a "classical" form of its own. The owner of a fine piece of eighteenth century horseflesh wanted it represented, as would his descendants to-day, with every "point" marked and hair in place. He did not want a picture of a horse, but a portrait of his own thoroughbred. George Stubbs, the greatest of those to fulfil this requirement, and one of the greatest anatomists of his age in addition, must have made literally thousands of drawings both for his pictures and for his celebrated literary "chef d'œuvre," *The Anatomy of the Horse.* When his effects were

THE CHIMNEY PIECE

Wash drawing by Henry Fuseli, 1741-1825

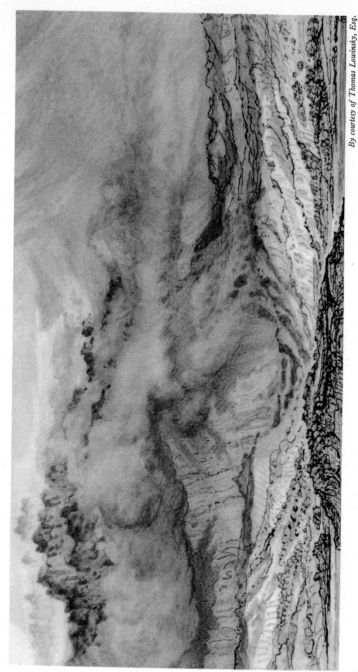

SNOWDON UNDER CLOUD

Pen and wash drawing by James Ward, 1853

auctioned after his death in 1806, four lots of sketchbooks were catalogued, one of which contained no less than 200 landscapes, another "12 monkeys, 14 Buffaloes Bulls and Cows, in black lead and two Tibet Bulls in black chalk." To-day the sum total of Stubbs' drawings amounts to a folio of pencil drawings in the Royal Academy, and one or two in the Picton Library, Liverpool. No others, I believe, are admitted by all the authorities. The change of fashion at the beginning of the nineteenth century, and consequent loss of interest in so eighteenth century an artist as Stubbs, was presumably the cause. As far as I know, none of his landscape drawings remain, in sad contrast to his contemporary, Thomas Gainsborough. Happily there is a very large number of Gainsborough's drawings in existence, as a result of the vogue for them that immediately followed his death. There are more extant, indeed, than by any of the artists so far discussed. The slender scope of this volume, therefore, makes it impossible to represent the development and change in Gainsborough's methods of drawing. As a portrait painter he was brilliantly gifted in catching a likeness and achieved a considerable success thereby. As a landscape draughtsman and in his casual figure studies, his work progressed from a manner derived from Van Dyke, whom he profoundly admired, to a simple, wonderfully controlled, almost impressionist method of notation in chalk and wash and charcoal heightened with white, which places him in the company of Constable as the greatest of all British landscape draughtsmen. His figure drawings suggest a comparison with Watteau, an artist whom he temperamentally resembles, in their elegance and economy of means, and early examples bear a considerable resemblance to the great Frenchman's chalk drawings as a result of the influence of Gainsborough's master, the French engraver, Hubert Gravelot, who owned some Watteau drawings which he prized above all else. There are, however, essential differences between Watteau and Gainsborough. Watteau loved the exquisitely artificial; Gainsborough disliked his portrait practice and loved natural landscape. During his life he casually gave away his drawings for, like his landscape paintings, they would not sell.

Where Gainsborough particularised, Sir Joshua Reynolds generalised. Reynolds' gifts were on a heroic scale, but linear sensitivity was not one of them. He concerned himself with being a great master and, by dint of his enormous energy, he succeeded, at least partially, in achieving his aim. As a draughtsman he has little to commend him in the comparatively few examples which survive. "The grand manner" was his goal, and drawing was not perhaps the medium most suited to this aim in the eighteenth century. The best of his drawings, most of which are in pen or pen and wash, have power and *bravura*, but Reynolds was an oil painter first and last.

With the notable exception of those already mentioned, our famous eighteenth and nineteenth century portraitists, Reynolds, Opie, Hoppner, and Lawrence, are not particularly interesting as draughtsmen, and the

THE SPIRIT OF GOD
Wash drawing by George Romney, 1734-1802

same stricture applies to the "history painters," Benjamin West, J. S. Copley, and that great autobiographer if third-rate artist, Benjamin Robert Haydon. British portraiture irrespective of art, was, of necessity, a matter of output. Portraits were commodities in great demand and portraiture was a sound profession, where other forms of art might be dangerously unremunerative. But individual prices were not high and oil paintings were the artifacts required, so to maintain a reputation as a portraitist, the artist was required to paint away in oils most of the time available. On the whole, therefore, the portrait painter's drawings were very subsidiary productions. George Romney was an exception, for he worked very fast and painted very badly. His drawings are far more interesting than his oils. This was due to some extent to his contact with the drawings of William Blake and being deeply affected by Blake's unique vision, but Romney was making imaginative drawings before he met Blake and the influence was to some extent mutual. To this whole visionary movement, which had Blake as its greatest and, at the time, most neglected exponent, I will refer in due course.

The eighteenth century is so crowded with talent that I must inevitably do less than justice to many admirable artists. The landscapists in watercolour, Samuel Scott, Francis Towne, William Pars and many others, I propose to omit on the grounds that they are sufficiently served elsewhere and are neither pure draughtsmen nor great masters. Paul Sandby deserves most attention for though he never produced a masterpiece, he did produce numerous followers and some very pleasant wash drawings in the manner of Gainsborough and Richard Wilson, whom he helped when the latter was very poor. His real gift lay in his ability to record everyday life without pretention and with rare taste. The great school of English water-colour and landscape painting which culminated in Girtin, Turner, Cotman, Bonington and others, owed much to Sandby and his contemporaries.

ASCENDANCY II

BRITISH drawing reaches its second ascendancy towards the end of the eighteenth century and in the first quarter of the nineteenth. For the seven years between 1757 and 1764, the greatest individual figures—Hogarth, Wilson, Gainsborough, Ramsay, Stubbs, Cozens, Blake and Rowlandson—were actually all alive at the same time. It is, for some reason or other, generally assumed that both William Blake and Thomas Rowlandson are early nineteenth century artists, but in actual fact, Blake was born in 1757 and his art is in one respect timeless, while Rowlandson was born a year earlier and his art is manifestly and splendidly temporal. Rowlandson's art stems from the popular tradition of satire and social comment which had produced Hogarth, though he was without his predecessor's morality. His drawings themselves were almost invariably made with a reed pen and wash or watercolour tint, and he never painted in oils, for all his drawings were either intended to be engraved or were set down for their own robust benefit. His production of drawings was as prodigious as his personal extravagance and he contrived to roister through his longish life without any apparent decline in his talent. The curious thing about Rowlandson is that whilst he is often "typed" as primarily a brutal caricaturist, he was really a lyrical artist full of joy, a satirist full of wit and laughter, but with very little real malice, who took life as he found it and is therefore very different from Hogarth and in no way to be confused with the bitter Gilray or the acid Cruikshank. He could produce monstrous caricatures of appalling ugliness but they have always about them the suggestion that they were merely done to annoy, like a schoolboy's drawing of "teacher" ; they are rarely tragic moralities. The immense vitality, the lyrical poetry of his landscapes, the rhythmic preoccupation, the social satire, combine to make in Rowlandson a sort of catalogue of all the trends save one in British drawing. He was strangely uninfluenced by the work of his contemporaries. If he was influenced by any one artist, it was by

Gainsborough, whose landscape conventions Rowlandson adapted to his own uses.

The one quality lacking in Rowlandson, the spiritual, is amply compensated for in William Blake who, as a draughtsman, had precious little else. The vast bulk of recent literature on the subject of Blake permits me to deal fairly briefly with him here. In my own personal and probably superstitious opinion, William Blake was one of the greatest beings ever to inhabit this planet, and had the Gods granted him a pictorial ability equal to his vision we should simply not know what he was about. The Gods did not, they made of him a competent engraver and a passable draughtsman. With these inadequate tools, by the sheer power of his imagination and some gift for designing within the picture, Blake contrived to make a unique contribution to European art. It is however important to correct the very general and mistaken impression that Blake was unique in the form his work took. Imaginative or visionary art was a going concern, with a number of able practitioners involved, in the latter half of the eighteenth century. No one of them was Blake's imaginative equal ; no one of them had anything approaching Blake's genius, but several of them

ENRAGED MAN
Pen drawing by Thomas Rowlandson, 1756-1827

28

THE ANCIENT OF DAYS
Drawing by William Blake, 1757-1827

drew better than Blake, from a technical point of view. All of them, both
his seniors and his juniors, now seem to radiate from Blake. They knew
him and their work achieved life; before they knew him they were comparatively empty; after his presence faded they dried up. George Romney,
twenty-three years Blake's senior, thought Blake's imaginative drawings
the equal of Michelangelo's and Romney had been at the same kind of
thing for some time. Henri Fuseli, sixteen years older than Blake, said he
was "damned good to steal from" and Fuseli was famous and pretty well
off, while Blake was considered mad and lived in poverty. The name of
John Flaxman, R.A., lives on in the light cast by Blake, rather than by his
own merits as a "neoclassical" sculptor and illustrator; and Blake's young
disciples—Samuel Palmer, George Richmond, Edward Calvert and John
Linnel—produced the work they are remembered by, in Blake's aura.
When this aura faded, they were one by one swallowed up by the second
Black Death, the industrial materialism of Victorian England, and were
heard of no more.

Those two great complements to one another, Rowlandson and Blake,
together possess all the qualities of this country's natural genius in drawing;
those qualities which we first see in the Winchester Bible. When they died,

29

both in the same year, their most talented followers and their traditions continued for half a decade and then gradually disappeared. George Cruikshank, for example, gave up drink and declined, social satire degenerated into the gentlemanly dullness of *Punch*, while Samuel Palmer took to respectable views of Italy and his power became vitiated.

The visionary school, if such they may be called, is worth attention as a very important phenomenon in British art. Its form was classical and Italianate, based on Raphael and Michelangelo in contrast to the prevailing mode for Dutch-derived picturesque naturalism. It was closely linked to literature and, in terms of the dicta of Roger Fry, is nothing more than "literary illustration," to be denigrated as such. In terms of reality it was one of the most significant phases of English art. Most of Blake's subjects are either illustrations to the Bible, Dante, Blair or Virgil, and others, or to his own poems. Fuseli concerned himself with Milton and Shakespeare, Romney's best drawings are illustrations to *Paradise Lost*, and Flaxman and Stothard were both primarily illustrators, the former particularly of the Greek epic poets. It is perhaps significant that almost all that remains of the great medieval period are "illustrations" to sacred books, because this "illustration" is the hallmark of a very considerable section of British art. Our literature is great enough, and our visual arts need take no shame in being a counterpart. Blake was the illuminator of his own prophetic books as Mathew Paris was the illustrator of his own prose. It is time that the word "literary" was relegated to the scrap heap of outmoded critical epithets, for half Europe's masterpieces are illustrations to the Bible, or the lives of the Saints.

Henri Fuseli, apart from his affinity with, and admiration for, Blake as a visionary romantic, provides something of a link between the supernormal symbolism of the latter and the fleshly vitality of that other aspect of our art associated with Rowlandson and the caricaturists; Fuseli was much interested in contemporary costume and manners and in the life around him, albeit he lent the ladies of his choice a slightly sinister air compatible with his feeling for the "pleasing horror" admired by Burke. Most people who have written of his period have dismissed Fuseli as melodramatic to the extent of being ridiculous, and without true depth. He is held up as a pasteboard Blake, surrounded by spurious spectres and "property" blood. I must beg to disagree. At times Fuseli was inclined to push his emotions too far and his cult of the supernatural may occasionally seem exaggerated to the sceptical agnostics of to-day, but Fuseli had genuine power, morbid though it may have been, and his best work is far more than an amusing relic of his period. He saw his contemporaries clearly if theatrically, which may also be said of El Greco.

Fuseli was a Swiss who came to England when he was twenty-two and spent most of his long life here. He was a major figure of the romantic visionary school and, as I said earlier, more English than anything else,

RUTH RETURNED FROM GLEANING
Chalk and wash drawing by Samuel Palmer, exhibited 1829

except in his accent, which remained obstinately broken. He spent some time in Rome, where, apart from deciding upon the permanent spelling of his name, which had been variously "Fussli," "Fussel" and "Fusseli" until then, he met an Edinburgh man called John Brown. Brown is as anonymous as his name implies. Very little is certainly known about him, but whether he had a decided influence on Fuseli's style or vice versa, Brown produced a number of drawings, in the manner now associated with Fuseli, which are in no way inferior in quality. Both Brown and Fuseli were more concerned with the immediate and even satirical view of their fellow humans than was Blake, or the Romney of the imaginative drawings, and as such they provide something of a link with Rowlandson and those artists whose exclusive concern with everyday life make them the reverse of Blake's coin.

The school of landscape painters who derived from Sandby, Crome and the great Thomas Girtin made their contribution essentially to water-colour and oil painting, to which their drawings are subsidiary. Turner was the culmination of this movement and Turner, though a magnificent pictorial designer, was not a draughtsman *per se*. His most interesting drawings are his rapid notes, for which he perfected a personal technique, using a toned paper and a brisk calligraphic line. There are no less than 350 of his sketchbooks in the national collection, covering a period of fifty-nine years, from the careful topography of his youth to the graphic shorthand of his later years. But most of his drawings, as opposed to his watercolour paintings, were for his personal use and not for publication. Exciting though they are as documents of his life and approach to paintings, they are not, in themselves, particularly impressive. John Constable's are, and with him I will deal more fully, while David Cox had an uneven flair for dramatic landscape drawing, which at its best was superb, deriving from the work of Alexander Cozens.

Of the animal artists who were still following their long tradition and plying their quiet trade, two were so outstanding as draughtsmen that they require very special consideration. Of these, one was James Ward, a curiously underrated artist to-day, an example of whose landscape drawings I repro- duce in colour. If this drawing fails to show the reader that Ward was a master, the loss is not Ward's. Ward lived to a very great age, and this, as is sometimes the case, was synonymous with loss of reputation, for he outlived his popularity. He was the brother-in-law of the now more cele- brated George Morland, whose work was treasured by nineteenth century collectors presumably because of its sentimentality and which even now fetches high prices. Ward made his living as an animal portraitist, at which practice he is almost the equal of Stubbs. Long before 1859, when he died at the age of ninety, the market for animal pictures had changed. The public wanted the sentimental "bow-wows" and "gee-gees" of Edwin Landseer, and Ward's dramatic, picturesque landscapes with bulls fighting and storms brewing were outmoded. Ward was one of the products of Burke's "Sublime and Beautiful" which required a note of terror to heighten the sublimity. This he combined, as did the natural landscape painters like Girtin and Constable, with an admiration for Dutch painting and with a particular love for Rubens. Like Constable, Ward drew from nature and he drew from it continuously, year in and year out, all through his long life. Combined with skill, sensitivity and a deep passion, this practice makes a man a fine draughtsman. This it did for James Ward.

Thomas Bewick's name is still famous to wood engravers, book collectors and students of fauna and wild life. His *History of British Birds* and his *British Quadrupeds* are classics in this branch of the arts. Very few of his exquisite drawings remain, though there are a number of water- colours in existence, but his powers as an engraver ably demonstrate the delicacy and minuteness of his observation. John Piper speaks of him in *British Romantic Artists* as being able to see "all human experience in a bird's nest"; and there is some truth in this, for in his tiny engravings, Bewick was a complete artist of exceptional power. His great gift was his ability to perceive essentials and to separate the object from its context

VIEW ON THE STOUR
Wash drawing by John Constable, c. 1820

as a thing perfect in itself. In the nutshell, the macrocosm which concerns many artists of our own day so deeply, Bewick "could count himself a king of infinite space."

John Constable, as a draughtsman, was the product of the Norwich school, of Dutch landscape painting and of Claude. He combined these derivations with a simple and passionate vision of nature which made him the greatest landscape draughtsman of his period and, with Gainsborough, the greatest exponent of the "natural picturesque" in British art. He used a somewhat similar technique to Gainsborough in his wash drawings, the vast majority of which are notations and preparations for paintings. He was forever recording the changes in nature, and in particular in the weather and the formation of clouds. Leslie, his biographer, quotes an exchange between Blake (whom he terms "the amiable but eccentric") and Constable, which at once gives the key to their two personalties. Blake, looking through one of Constable's sketchbooks, was so moved by a drawing of trees that he exclaimed, "Why this is not drawing but inspiration"; to which Constable replied, "I never knew it before; I meant it for drawing." These two seemingly incompatible spirits shared something, but to Blake all art was "inspiration," whilst Constable said that when he made a sketch from nature the first thing he tried to do was to forget that he had ever seen a

33

picture. Nevertheless, these apparent antitheses with which we are presented in the late eighteenth and early nineteenth centuries are not really so incompatible as they seem. These artists were all, the greatest of them, "lyrical romantics," by which is meant, men who see reality where others see pictures. No matter how different their art seems on the surface to be, Gainsborough, Blake, Rowlandson, Constable, Ward, Bewick and Turner possessed that one common quantity which is found in the work of their great ancestors, the draughtsmen of Winchester and Canterbury. Blake and Rowlandson in particular are diverse but clear instances of the British gift for linear rhythm, found in the Cædmon MS. and in the work of Mathew Paris.

Constable is the final expression in this country of the "picturesque natural" school of landscape draughtsmen. Those who followed him in this direction never achieved his stature. His direct influence on English painting and drawing is still present in the work of Philip Wilson Steer and a host of less interesting and now archaic landscapists, but it was in France, in the work of Delacroix, and more obviously in that of Courbet and his followers, that the real heritage of Constable may be seen, together with that of R. P. Bonington, who spent most of his short life there. Three hundred years before Constable's day, we had passed the flower of our culture to France, and it was to France in the 1830's that we handed the fruits of our eighteenth century renaissance. The decline in the early nineteenth century led to no such complete wilderness in the Victorian era as did its historical parallel in the reign of Henry VIII. There was no complete cessation of activity ; far from it. Throughout the nineteenth century there were a number of excellent British draughtsmen, but a decline there was, as everyone knows, and if, as I believe, we may to-day be rising slowly from it to another period of ascendancy there is no evidence as yet of an artist to rank with the greatest of the eighteenth and early nineteenth century masters. In the 1820's and 30's there were draughtsmen like the Varleys and Samuel Palmer who were doing their best work and who were destined to sink into insignificance under the weight of the Victorian demand for sentiment and false naturalism, but in Palmer's youth, Blake, Constable, Turner and Rowlandson were still alive and there was still great vitality in British art. It was not until the 50's that the downhill course was truly run. Of Palmer so much has recently been written that I will not retell the tale of his shortlived period of supreme excellence. Suffice that it is Palmer, more than any other individual draughtsman, who influences the landscape drawing of the younger generation to-day. He was an artist in whose best work may be found the complete expression, in landscape, of Blake's teaching and example. Palmer's debt to Blake's woodcuts for Thornton's translation of Virgil's *Eclogues* is a case in point. Palmer was a creator of poetic landscapes ranking with those of Constable and Gainsborough, but in a completely different form.

ROCKY COAST WITH PORT
Pen and water-colour drawing by Richard Dadd, 1861

DECLINE AND DESERT II

THE early years of Queen Victoria's reign were years of great technical advance in the tools of the draughtsman's trade. The steel pen-nib was comparatively new and various types were being produced which had, of course, a considerable effect on the quality of line in subsequent drawings. "The metal pen," to quote Hesketh Hubbard, "made possible a thinner, more flexible line than the reed or quill usually produced. This was not entirely beneficial, for though it made possible greater delicacy and detail, it also encouraged a spidery, wiry line that lacked decorative value." This is an understatement. Even Rossetti, the best of the Pre-Raphaelite draughtsmen, steel pen and all, had not at his command the flexibility of line to be found in the Winchester Bible, nor had Maclise's fiddling the delicacy of Hillyarde. The Victorians confused superfluity of detail with delicacy, to the lengths of that nadir of all drawing, the "stipple landscape." New papers and new tones of paper were marketed in great numbers, such as those named after Cotman, Harding and Cattermole. The lead pencil was perfected, and in fact everything possible to simplify the mechanics of drawing was made available to the aspiring student. Given

WOMAN ON A SOFA
Pen drawing by Sir David Wilkie, 1805

36

SPANISH MODEL
Pen drawing by Charles Keene, 1823-1891

the tools, they failed to do the job, though not for want of finish. The rising
stars of popular esteem, destined for honours and peerages, Landseer,
Leighton, Poynter, and others, managed to produce little beside abysmal
sentimentalities of a high level of competence (though Landseer in particular was a gifted artist) compatible with the false values of the spurious
"neo-Gothic"; a mode unrelated to our own genuine Gothic tradition.
The gallant but unsuccessful Pre-Raphaelite reaction from the "neo-Gothic"

37

MISS FANNY CORNFORTH
Pen and wash drawing by Dante Gabriel Rossetti, 1828-1882

factory chimney actually did much good, doomed though even this was by false, though far less false, values, this time the understandable but fruitless archaism inherent in the title "Pre-Raphaelite." While the officials tried to bring the "Gothic" up-to-date, the Pre-Raphaelites tried to take the public back to the Gothic past. Confusion arose. One way and another, the Victorian era managed, with the best of intentions, to negate and stultify the lyrical romantic part of the indigenous expression, gifted though many of the individual protagonists were. As before, it was left in the hands of one section of the tradition to keep the torch alight. In this case it was the social commentators and the illustrators.

Before plunging into the densely populated undergrowth of Victorian draughtsmen, I should like to consider one lunatic artist and one artist whose brothers were both mad. The first is the sad figure of Richard Dadd, for so long underrated, and shortly to be so overrated. Dadd was trained at the Academy schools, and all his life practised a tight, detailed mode of expression. Had he not, as a result of a sunstroke sustained in Egypt, killed his father with a razor, he might well have continued in the fairly prosperous and modest course of an ordinary academic artist. Instead, contingent upon his lethal pun, he was judged insane in 1843 and spent the rest of his life in Bedlam and Broadmoor where he produced a fantastic art quite unique in British drawing, executed with a miniaturist's detail which foreshadowed the technique of the Pre-Raphaelites of a decade later. Dadd, like Blake, was "eccentric," but differed not only in that his talents were less, but also in that presumably he was not "amiable." The other, John Martin, was not confined in any way, on the contrary he was a very great success. His paintings and engravings occasionally, as in his *Paradise Lost* illustrations, achieve considerable scenic magnificence by dint of his sense of scale, but his art was pure theatre and technically, though he was a fine engraver, he was rather a niggling draughtsman. Martin, like Dadd, comes as a pendant to the melodramatic aspect of the visionary school. Both of them pushed on from Fuseli, whether they knew it or not, into the hinterland of lunacy.

NIGHT PIECE
Pen and brush drawing by Aubrey Beardsley, 1872-1898

39

Martin was sane and an anticlimax, a *reductio ad absurdum*. Dadd was mad and achieved a curious purity as a result.

The social commentators who were to hold the structure of British drawing together divide into two classes, upper and lower, but mainly upper. David Wilkie, Andrew Geddes, John Tenniel, Charles Keene, John Leech, Richard Doyle, W. P. Frith, and later Aubrey Beardsley and Max Beerbohm mostly drew for the benefit of the upper classes, unlike Rowlandson and Gilray, who drew for anyone possessing a sixpence. Of these Keene, Leech, Doyle and Frith drew the lower classes for the benefit of the upper and Tenniel, Beardsley and "Max" drew the upper classes in one kind or another for the benefit of their intellectual or social peers and themselves. Wilkie was a highly talented draughtsman but a second-rank painter of what are called *genre* pictures. This means, the faithful recording, in greater or less degree, of one's immediate surroundings and acquaintances. Wilkie put down what he saw, boldly but unpretentiously, leaving behind him a pleasant and instructive record of his times, and a number of powerful drawings. W. P. Frith is also a draughtsman of this type, but coming, as he did, at a later and more desolate period, his work is crowded with pretentious sentimentalities and superfluous detail. Leech and Keene differ from Wilkie in that they were humorists and therefore had an *arrière-pensée*. Charles Keene is unquestionably the leading native draughtsman of the mid-nineteenth century, to the extent of actual greatness, but he recorded rather than created and though a master draughtsman and a sensitive artist gifted with much human understanding, he only rose above first-rate journalism in his finest work. His friend John Tenniel had less talent but a vein of delicate fantasy which makes it impossible for anyone else ever to illustrate *Alice in Wonderland*. His political cartoons are well drawn and very gentlemanly. The art of social satire became very well-mannered in Victoria's reign, as *Punch* shows only too well. It was sometimes not without wit but it was always lacking in the savage emotions of the many ferociously angry satirical draughtsmen of earlier in the century. Emotions and particularly social emotions except in support of the *status quo* were not welcome in the 60's. However, in Keene's hands, and to some extent in the others', drawing was still drawing, as Sickert was at pains to point out in our own day and as Sickert's own drawings show, in his debt to Keene. In the hands of the famous painters it was not. They drew by measurement and by preconceived rules. Whilst this respectably dreary state of affairs proceeded along the years, John Ruskin, who had championed Turner—rather to the latter's embarrassment—began to campaign with all the might of his prose for the young men who were trying to rid themselves of the spiritual grime of the Industrial Revolution. He came out hot and strong for the Pre-Raphaelites, and Ruskin, unlike our contemporary midget critics, had spirit and carried a certain amount of weight, if not as much as is generally supposed in retrospect. But in addition, Ruskin was

JOACHIM AMONG THE SHEPHERDS
Pen and wash drawing by Stanley Spencer, 1912
By courtesy of the Artist and Miss Lillian Browse

TWO SISTERS
Drawing in coloured chalks by Robert Colquhoun, 1945

quite a respectable draughtsman himself. The Pre-Raphaelites, among them John Everett Millais, who metamorphosed from a brilliantly talented rebel into a wealthy and reactionary dispenser of saccharine platitudes, and Dante Gabriel Rossetti, a fine draughtsman and a great poet, were launched as a movement and were soon set upon by the wits and social commentators —the other good draughtsmen—as suitable grist to the mill of graphic wit. Draughtsmen were at pains to eat draughtsmen. Whilst this scrimmage was going on, certain individuals were proceeding quietly with their own work. The illustrators "Phiz" (Hablot Knight Browne) and the younger Cruikshank were established and were, with younger men such as Noel Paton, G. J. Pinwell, A. B. Frost and many more, building book illustration into the one visual product of the Victorian era which had real life. The topographers Samuel Prout, George Cattermole and W. H. Bartlett were quietly continuing the slightly tedious tradition of the picturesque ruin, which dawdled on almost into the twentieth century. Several adventurous spirits had wandered into the Near, and one into the Far, East. Of these the best are John Frederick Lewis, called "Spanish Lewis," Edward Lear, the celebrated creator of much sublime nonsense and a good deal of less celebrated but admirable straight landscape drawing in Italy, Palestine and thereabouts ; and George Chinnery who really belongs to an earlier generation and who lived the greater part of his life in India and China. Lewis, who was a superb technician, spent his time in Turkey and Egypt, working in the now perfected medium of pencil of which he possessed a complete mastery, and making lithographs of a high degree of intensity. His drawings of animals make him the major figure in this field after James Ward. Lear's lyrical gift is discernible in all his work, comic and serious, and his drawings of birds are of an exceptional quality. George Chinnery was an artist of quiet ability and very real insight, whose drawings of Chinese types are more than a valuable record of the country and the era. The divers draughtsmen, illustrators, topographers and the rest, are the real, almost the only artistic fruits of the age. Painting and sculpture were either ineffectual or deplorable, but drawing continued doggedly to keep its end up in some sort. Alfred Stevens, a grandiose practitioner in the arts of painting, architecture, sculpture and general decoration, was a carefully trained artist in all that was "traditional" in the Greco-Roman manner current in his time. The fact remains that he was a superficial and facile draughtsman of very little value to his contemporaries, though he has gained something of a reputation since, for reasons best known to the dealers.

The memory of Blake, dim but persistent, lights some aspects of the mid-nineteenth century. Rossetti was a profound admirer, Noel Paton's masterpiece, the *Ancient Mariner* illustrations, has echoes of Blake and the Pre-Raphaelite books follow his example of individual craftsmanship in book production. Moxon's editions of *Tennyson* and *Poets of the Nine-teenth Century* with illustrations by Rossetti, Millais, the wretched Holman

41

Hunt, victim of a retarded development which, had he lived two hundred years, would not have prevented him from becoming a great artist, and Ford Madox Brown who, in another age, would have been one—were in their time something new and important in the craft of book production, though the editions were an expensive failure and reached only a small section of the public. The book, in the hands of the Pre-Raphaelites, may now seem over-ornamented and false in sentiment, but to William Morris, to several of the other Pre-Raphaelites, and even to the dreary Edward Burne-Jones, we owe the resurrection from long neglect of the great books and manuscripts of the eleventh and twelfth centuries, and the attempt to recreate the book as a work of art. That pre-Raphaelitism was an aesthetic failure based on false theorising, is acknowledged, but we owe something to individuals associated with the movement, Rossetti and Morris in particular, and in its time it was full of courage and had much that was true in its cause. That it was a flop in its unreal, quasi-medieval romanticism must be admitted, but the Pre-Raphaelites were fighting a more stubborn philistinism than England had suffered since the Commonwealth. It is not surprising therefore that they spoilt their case by overstating it.

RESURRECTION II

THE gift to France, made in the earlier years of the nineteenth century, began to return to this country towards the end of the 1870's, under the auspices of that arrogant and intelligent product of French Impressionism and the Japanese print, James McNeill Whistler. Whistler does not come within the scope of this book since he was an American, who drew English subjects, in a French manner, with a Japanese feeling, and withal he drew rather badly. But Whistler talked the British into a realisation of what was then going on in France, and, at the time, this was a breath of fresh air blowing through this country's stuffy, overcrowded houses and studios. In this civilising mission he was assisted by all the ignorance at George Moore's command and all the glittering, sensitive nonsense of Oscar Wilde's avid love of novelty. Three British draughtsmen rapidly, though not entirely relevantly, followed this vocal rather than graphic revolution. The first is the personification of the period in literature, that astonishing and shortlived artist, Aubrey Vincent Beardsley. Beardsley was born in 1872 and died of tuberculosis in 1898. Between 1893 and his death he produced a considerable body of highly original and artificial drawings, designed expressly for line block reproduction, which set England and most of Europe by the ears. His work was intensely literary, to the extent of being, not just illustration but an integral part of a book, as integral as the capital letters, but it was also a social comment on the appearance of one fragment of the times in which he lived. Beardsley had no particular talent as a draughtsman of form, nor any particular virtue

SEATED WOMAN
Pen and wash drawing by Wyndham Lewis

of line, but what he did have was a wonderful sense of balancing white against black and a morbid, personal vision. His *nostalgie de la boue parfumée* was exactly suited to the jewelled escapism of the literature of his period, the transitory epoch of the "decadents." Beardsley arrived at the right moment and he knew when to leave. Max Beerbohm, who happily was much the same age then as now, is a far more skilful draughtsman than his drawings, slight, elegant satirical comments on celebrated con-

43

THE LONDON, SHOREDITCH
Pencil drawing by Walter Sickert, 1860-1942

temporaries, would have one suppose. They seem intentionally ephemeral; in actual fact they are much more. The third of the draughtsmen whose work emerges from this period is Walter Richard Sickert, who combined a pastiche of Degas and Whistler in paint with a magnificent graphic gift, descending directly from Keene and as native as a London fog. Sooner or later it will transpire that Sickert's drawings were far and away the most important part of his production and then they will be seen in their true light as illustrations of a period and not only as studies for impressionist painting.

The impact of French art in the 90's and in the first ten years of the twentieth century gave birth to a lively movement associated with the Slade School and the New English Art Club which was founded, as are most of such groups, in order to exhibit the work of talented rebels at odds with the R.A. Philip Wilson Steer, Sickert, and among the younger men, Ambrose MacEvoy, William Orpen and Augustus John are the most important names associated with it. Orpen was brilliantly

STUDY OF A FISHERGIRL OF EQUIHEN
Pencil drawing by Augustus John

endowed, but after a good start he degenerated into an Academic slickness which requires no further comment. John's reputation as a draughtsman is so extensive that it needs no recapitulation here. In the Edwardian era, James Pryde and William Nicholson as "The Beggarstaff Brothers" produced posters and drawings for woodcuts which attracted considerable attention, and the Scotsmen, D. Y. Cameron and Muirhead Bone were producing traditional landscape drawings mainly with a view to etching. Charles Rickets and Charles Shannon were the most celebrated illustrators and the Slade School reached its peak in the production of John, Orpen and Wyndham Lewis.

The resurrection which took place in the early eighteenth century seems sudden in retrospect and almost miraculous. The late nineteenth century, and the course of twentieth century drawing so far, has been a far more gradual development with, as will be seen, a fairly large number of diverse practitioners in action concurrently. The decline from greatness which followed the deaths of Constable and Turner was sharp, but the line continued in a gradual curve which began to rise imperceptibly in the 90's, was faced with a relapse as a result of the wild Francophilia of the cosmopolitan "twenties" and early thirties, and is now moving up again. The "Vorticist" movement of the hectic period shortly before 1914 brought Wyndham Lewis to the fore as perhaps the greatest living British portrait draughtsman, and produced William Roberts, whose metallic figure drawings have considerable power. At much the same time, the mystical realism of Stanley Spencer's early figure drawings and, in landscape, the work of Paul Nash began to show the first signs of re-emergence of the native tradition in a pure state. In the 'twenties, as a result of Roger Fry's admirable realisation of the significance of Post-Impressionism being pushed too far, false and hysterical trends based on the multifarious movements contained in the *Ecole de Paris* eclipsed the growing tendency to recognise the value of the indigenous tradition, in a Mediterranean fluorescence which did inestimable damage to the roots of certain very talented artists. Marc Gertler was one who suffered from false cosmopolitanism, to some extent Christopher Wood was another, though he redeemed himself towards the end of his brief life, and there are several more who fared equally badly. It was not until the 'thirties that the camps could be seen more evenly divided, and not until the Second World War that the direction was clearly taken by the younger generation in spite of the opposition from the Francophiles.

I have not space here to document the considerable body of draughtsmen who are British in the sense that they are aware of their tradition, nor can I tabulate the conflicting influences present in their work, over and above their artistic nationality. The French masters, and of course the towering single figure of Picasso, have left their mark, beneficial and otherwise, on all contemporary painting and drawing. What I shall do in ending this essay, is to restate what I consider to be the main streams or characteristics of the British genius, the lyrical, the satiric, the mystical, the romantic and the preoccupation with linear rhythms, which are the bones and basis of our art, and have been so for a thousand years, and to name my own choice of those whom I think figure most significantly in this tradition to-day. Of the generation which follows the lyrical romanticism of Paul Nash, follows in time rather than in direct derivation, Graham Sutherland —the artistic descendant of Blake, Samuel Palmer, Cozens and Turner— seems to me the most important, for the vital paraphrase of landscape forms at which he has arrived through drawing. Edward Bawden, whose vision is of a gentler sort, stems through Nash from Edward Lear and recalls Bewick and Barlow in his approach rather than in his subject matter. The drawings of David Jones are a symbol of the continuity of tradition. They bear a strong family resemblance to the first colour plate in this book— not that they are archaic, but in their lyrical, linear freedom. His animal drawings and his engravings only serve to emphasise this fact for they are in the tradition of British animal drawing so consistently excellent throughout the centuries. Frances Hodgkins is another fine lyrical artist of the

ORCHARD
Pen and wash drawing by John Minton, 1945

younger generation in all save her actual age. Edward Burra looked back to Rowlandson and Hogarth and he is, with Spencer, the major visual satirist of to-day. Henry Moore, the sculptor, deserves mention here for a few of the best of his numerous drawings and so does John Piper, who follows the tradition of Cotman and the topographers, though neither of them is outstanding as draughtsman. Of an even younger generation still, I reproduce a chalk drawing by Robert Colquhoun and a landscape in pen and wash by John Minton. Colquhoun's roots are in that Celtic gift for design mentioned at the beginning of this book and his origins as an artist go back to the Northumbrian illuminators. Minton is English and Palmer shines through him, but his work is personal none the less. These are two from among several young artists whose work in due time will become familiar.

It has not been my intention to propound a specious archaism nor to advocate a bigoted parochialism. I do not think that any of the last four reproductions in this book will convey the impression that the present British school displays antiquarian or over-insular tendencies. Trying to go back may have been the downfall of the Pre-Raphaelites, awareness of one's native tradition is another thing. It is my belief that the value of our long tradition is such that it can help to produce, in the not too distant future, a new renaissance in British art and thus a new national culture to put into the international pool of European art. If this is achieved it will be through drawing, for that is our natural mode of visual expression.

My chapter headings read as a cycle. If this great wheel continues to turn, the chapter yet to be written will be ASCENDANCY No. III.

THORNTREE
Pen and wash drawing by Graham Sutherland, 1945

SHORT BIBLIOGRAPHY

Early Medieval Art in the British Museum by Ernst Kitzinger. British Museum Publication, 1940.—*The Artists of the Winchester Bible* by W. Oakeshott. Faber 1945. —*England and the Mediterranean Tradition*, The Courtauld and Warburg Institutes. Oxford University Press, 1946.—*English Painting* by R. H. Wilenski. Faber 1943.— *Hogarth and British Caricature*. Transatlantic Arts, 1944.—*Commemorative Catalogue of the Exhibition of British Art at Burlington House*. Oxford Press, 1935.—*English Watercolours* by Laurence Binyon. A. & C. Black, 1944.—*The Followers of William Blake* by Laurence Binyon. Halton, Truscott & Smith, 1925.—*Some Victorian Draughtsmen* by Hesketh Hubbard. Cambridge Press, 1944.—*British Romantic Artists* by John Piper. Britain in Pictures, 1942